Thanks to the creative team:
Senior Editor: Alice Peebles
Fact checking: Kate Mitchell
Design: www.collaborate.agency

Original edition copyright 2016 by Hungry Tomato Ltd.

Copyright © 2017 by Lerner Publishing Group, Inc.

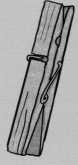

Hungry Tomato™ is a trademark of Lerner Publishing Group, Inc.

Hungry Tomato™
A division of Lerner Publishing Group, Inc.
241 First Avenue North
Minneapolis, MN 55401 USA

For reading levels and more information, look up this title at www.lernerbooks.com.

Main body text set in Bodoni 72.
Typeface provided by International Typeface Corp.

Library of Congress Cataloging-in-Publication Data

The Cataloging-in-Publication Data for *Ready, Aim, Launch!: Make Your Own Small Launchers* is on file at the Library of Congress.
ISBN 978-1-5124-0636-8 (lib. bdg.)
ISBN 978-1-5124-1173-7 (pbk.)
ISBN 978-1-5124-0923-9 (EB pdf)

Manufactured in the United States of America
1-39309-21146-5/2/2016

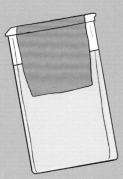

TABLETOP WARS
READY, AIM, LAUNCH!
Make Your Own Small Launchers

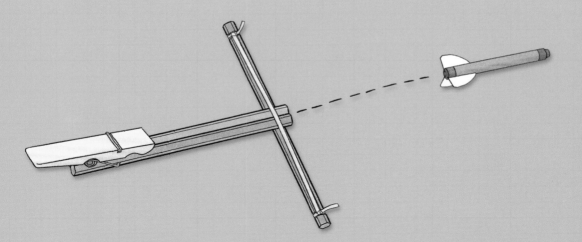

by Rob Ives
Illustrated by John Paul de Quay

HUNGRY TOMATO™

Minneapolis

Safety First!

Take care and use good sense when making these small launchers. Even though the models are small and use missiles with blunted ends and candy ammunition, the unexpected can happen. When building and using the launchers, be responsible and always be safe.

Bolts, darts, and other missiles can cause damage when fired with force. Never point the launchers or aim anything at people, animals, or anything of value.

Look for the safety warning sign in the activities and ask an adult for assistance when you are cutting materials.

Watch for this sign throughout the book. You may need help from an adult to complete these tasks.

CONTENTS

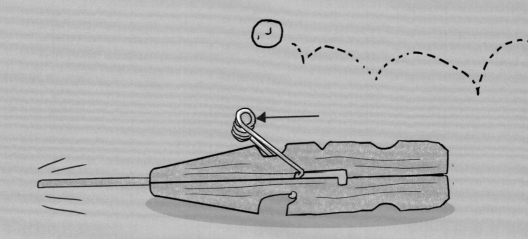

SMALL LAUNCHERS

This book shows you how to make small, fun launchers inspired by eight small weapons used in traditional warfare, medieval battles, and beyond. Cut, glue, and get ready for a surprise attack!

Supply List:

To make the amazing launchers in this book, you will need these supplies. Most items can be found at home, school, or a craft store:

Thick Drinking Straws

Thin Card

Adhesive Putty

Cotton Thread

Wooden Clothespins

Coffee Stirrers

Wooden Craft Sticks

Pencils

Plastic Pen with Round Barrel

Rubber Bands

Pencil Eraser

Large Wooden Skewers, 12 inches (30.5 cm) long

Wax Crayon

MINT

Plastic Mint Box

Mints

Small Wooden Skewers, 4 inches (10 cm) long

Small Launchers

This is a fun guide to making simple miniature launchers from everyday items. The devices that inspired them come from different historic times, but are mainly early or medieval inventions. All used different methods of shooting an object at an enemy or their defenses. These mini-versions deliver rubber bands or candy across the room!

So, dig into your drawers and cabinets for the few items you will need, and exercise your fingers and your brain. The projects can be made in multiples, too, so are great to make with friends. And remember, before you start, to read the safety tips on page 4, and look out for the safety warning sign where you'll need a little adult help. So get ready, aim, and launch!

TIPS

Some projects ask for pencils to be cut into sections. Ask for help with this and use a cutting mat to cut on. An efficient way to do this is to cut each face of the pencil and then snap it apart. Tidy up any unevenness with a craft knife.

Also ask for help with cutting the barrel of a pen—this can be quite tricky!

Tools Needed:

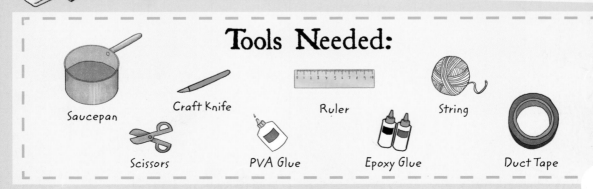

Saucepan   Craft Knife   Ruler   String

Scissors   PVA Glue   Epoxy Glue   Duct Tape

CRAYON LAUNCHER

This launcher was inspired by the crossbow, an ancient Chinese invention that was later used by medieval warriors. See how rubber band power sends a crayon flying across the room with this launcher.

Supplies:

Pencils x 3

Wax Crayon

Wooden Clothespin

Thin Card
4 x 4 inches (10 x 10 cm)

Tools:

Scissors   Craft Knife   PVA Glue   Ruler

Rubber Band

Instructions
STAGE 1

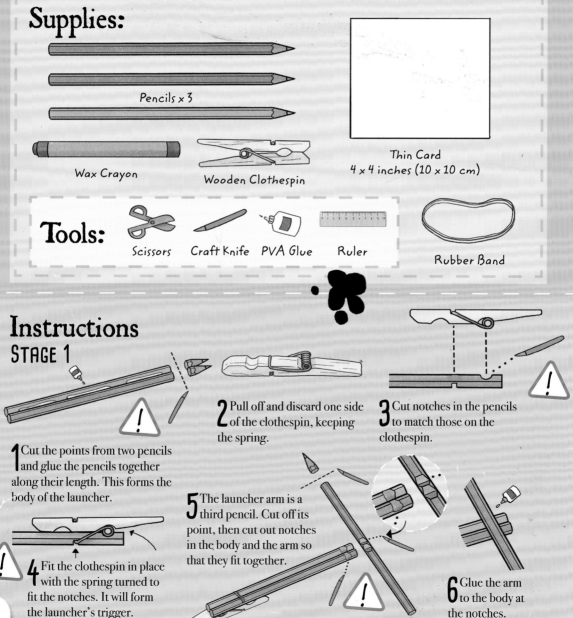

1 Cut the points from two pencils and glue the pencils together along their length. This forms the body of the launcher.

2 Pull off and discard one side of the clothespin, keeping the spring.

3 Cut notches in the pencils to match those on the clothespin.

4 Fit the clothespin in place with the spring turned to fit the notches. It will form the launcher's trigger.

5 The launcher arm is a third pencil. Cut off its point, then cut out notches in the body and the arm so that they fit together.

6 Glue the arm to the body at the notches.

8

STAGE 2

7 A crossbow launches arrows called bolts. The bolts for this launcher are crayons. Cut three notches in the crayon (bolt) to receive the flights. These are winglike pieces that help the bolt fly.

8 Cut and shape three flights 0.7 x 0.3 inch (2 x 1 cm) from the thin card. Glue the flights into the notches.

STAGE 3

9 Cut a notch at each end of the launcher arm. Cut a rubber band so it is one long piece.

10 Tie the rubber band to the notches, so it is just slightly stretched in this position.

11 Pull the rubber band back to fit under the trigger. Position the bolt in front of the trigger. Then release the clothespin to fire!

Launch!

MEDIEVAL CROSSBOW

The crossbow was set horizontally on a grooved stick called a stock. It had a mechanism to hold the bowstring tight. It was easy to use. Crossbowmen protected infantry and often preceded attacks by mounted knights.

PAPER DART LAUNCHER

Blowpipes were once used in South America and Southeast Asia to shoot poison darts. Try this version, which launches paper darts.

Supplies:

Cotton Thread

Thick Drinking Straw

Thin Card, 1.25 x 5 inches (3 x 12 cm)

Tools:

Ruler

Scissors

PVA Glue

Instructions

STAGE 1

1 Spread out your fingers on one hand. Wrap the thread fifteen times around your fingers to make a loop.

2 Cut the thread at one end of the loop.

STAGE 2

3 Cut a strip of card 1.25 x 5 inches (3 x 12 cm) with a tab at the end (as shown). Hang the thread over the tab.

4 Fold the tab into the card. Roll the card around the thread, leaving the loose ends free. These ends stabilize the dart in flight.

5 Glue down the edge of the card and trim the threads to the same length. Pull out the tube's layers at the other end so it tapers. This is the dart.

STAGE 3

6 Fit the dart inside the straw, enclosing the threads. Only push it in about 2 inches (5 cm) from the end of the straw. Then, blow!

Ready!
Aim!
Launch!

TRADITIONAL BLOWPIPES

Blowpipes were made from lengths of cane or bamboo, or were hollowed out of wood. The darts might be notched so they broke off in the victim. They carried poisonous sap, snake venom, insect or plant toxins, or rotted flesh.

RUBBER BAND LAUNCHER

Any good pirate always had a flintlock pistol with him. This project was inspired by the pirate's weapon, but launches rubber bands instead.

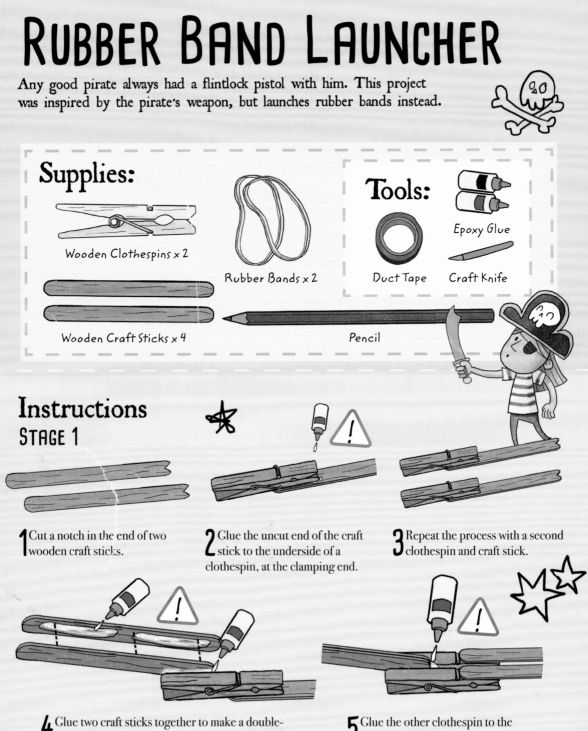

Supplies:

Wooden Clothespins x 2

Rubber Bands x 2

Wooden Craft Sticks x 4

Pencil

Tools:

Duct Tape

Epoxy Glue

Craft Knife

Instructions
STAGE 1

1 Cut a notch in the end of two wooden craft sticks.

2 Glue the uncut end of the craft stick to the underside of a clothespin, at the clamping end.

3 Repeat the process with a second clothespin and craft stick.

4 Glue two craft sticks together to make a double-thickness stick. Glue this piece to the long arm of one of the clothespins, lining it up with the edge of the clothespin as shown.

5 Glue the other clothespin to the other side. Make sure everything lines up. (Clothespins are shown turned over here.)

STAGE 2

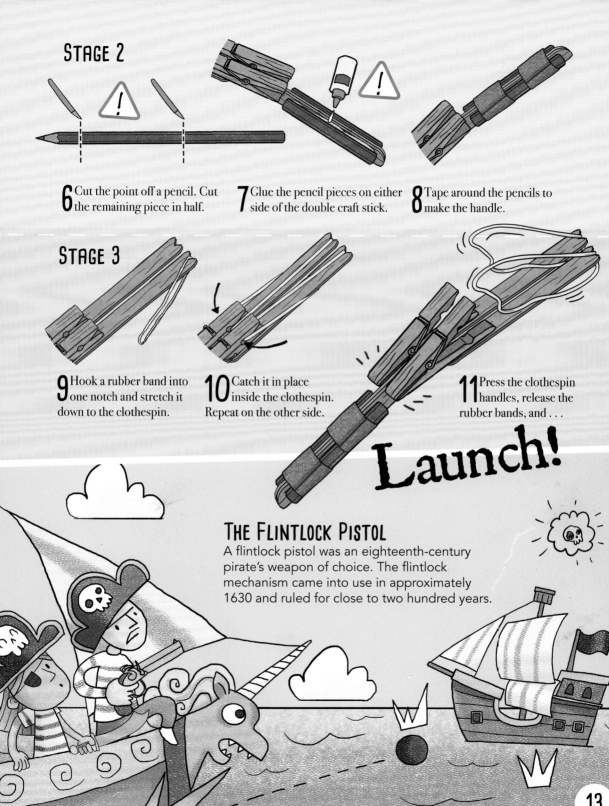

6 Cut the point off a pencil. Cut the remaining piece in half.

7 Glue the pencil pieces on either side of the double craft stick.

8 Tape around the pencils to make the handle.

STAGE 3

9 Hook a rubber band into one notch and stretch it down to the clothespin.

10 Catch it in place inside the clothespin. Repeat on the other side.

11 Press the clothespin handles, release the rubber bands, and . . .

Launch!

THE FLINTLOCK PISTOL

A flintlock pistol was an eighteenth-century pirate's weapon of choice. The flintlock mechanism came into use in approximately 1630 and ruled for close to two hundred years.

13

EXPLODING NINJA STAR

Ninja stealth warriors once used star-shaped throwing weapons. Try making your own exploding ninja star just by combining coffee stirrers.

Supplies:

Coffee Stirrers x 5

Instructions

Assemble the star by following the five steps in the pictures, no glue needed! Throw the star with a flick of the wrist and watch it explode on impact.

1

2

3

4

Throw!

JAPANESE *SHURIKEN*

Ninja never encumbered themselves with heavy weapons—they couldn't have done their secret work that way. Instead, they carried small throwing weapons called *shuriken*. These many-pointed metal stars might disable foes, or at least confuse them before an attack.

ROCKET LAUNCHER

Make a rocket launcher inspired by the *bohiya*, an early Japanese fire arrow launched from a handheld device. Use a strong burst of air from your lungs to set the rocket flying from this launcher.

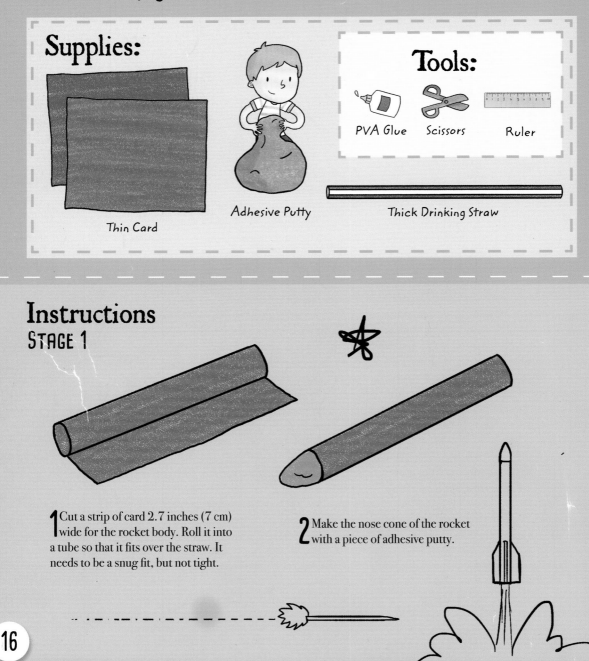

Supplies:

Thin Card

Adhesive Putty

Thick Drinking Straw

Tools:

PVA Glue   Scissors   Ruler

Instructions
STAGE 1

1 Cut a strip of card 2.7 inches (7 cm) wide for the rocket body. Roll it into a tube so that it fits over the straw. It needs to be a snug fit, but not tight.

2 Make the nose cone of the rocket with a piece of adhesive putty.

3 Cut and shape three flights from thin card, each 0.7 x 0.7 inches (2 x 2 cm). Fold back a tab 0.2 inch (0.5 cm) in from each straight edge.

4 Curve the tabs to fit the rocket body. Space the flights evenly around the rocket's end. Glue them in place.

5 Push the rocket onto one end of the straw. Then blow into the other end to launch the rocket.

Ready!
Aim!
Launch!

JAPANESE BOHIYA

Around 900 CE, the Chinese invented the fire arrow—actually a flammable rocket attached to the shaft of an arrow. The Japanese later made their version, called the bohiya. Samurai warriors launched it in various ways to set a distant target on fire. At first it was fired from a bow, and later from a rifle called a *hiya zutsu*. By the sixteenth century, the Japanese navy fired bohiya at enemy ships to set them on fire.

LAMINATED BOW

Try launching rubber-tipped skewers with this bow inspired by the medieval longbow. The original was once used by powerful archers on the battlefields of Europe.

Supplies:

Pencil Eraser

Wooden Craft Sticks x 6

Thin Card

Rubber Band

Wooden Clothespins

Large Wooden Skewer

Tools:

String   Epoxy Glue   Saucepan   PVA Glue   Craft Knife   Scissors   Ruler

Instructions
STAGE 1

1 Boil at least six craft sticks in water for five minutes to soften them. Drain and allow sticks to cool. Alternatively, you can soak them overnight. Choose the five most flexible craft sticks; keep the others as spares.

2 Use a cool saucepan to form the shape of the bow. While still wet, curve the five craft sticks in a double layer around the top edge of the saucepan. Make the sticks overlap evenly. Glue them together as you go.

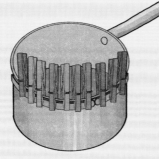

3 Pin the sticks in place around the top of the pan using clothespins. Leave overnight to dry completely. This makes the bow.

4 Once dry, unclamp the bow.

STAGE 2

5 Cut and shape the ends of the bow to make notches (as shown).

6 Mix PVA glue with an equal amount of water to make close to 2 tablespoons (25 mL). Soak 3 feet (1 m) of string in the mixture.

STAGE 3

7 Starting from one-third of the way along the bow, wrap the damp string tightly around it. Secure the end of the string by wrapping over it.

8 Wrap string to an equal point at the bow's other end. Tie off the string. As it dries, the string will shrink slightly and tightly grip the bow.

9 Tie a length of cut rubber band at the notches to complete the bow. Cut off the ends of the rubber band.

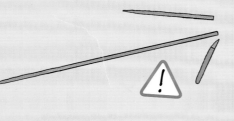

10 Cut a 4.5-inch (12-cm) length from the skewer to make the arrow.

11 Cut the eraser from a pencil to cover the skewer's point. Make a hole in the eraser with the skewer.

12 Use epoxy glue to secure the skewer to the eraser.

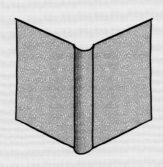

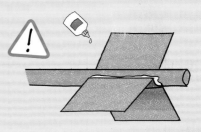

13 For the flights, cut three parallelogram shapes from thin card, roughly 0.7 x 0.3 inches (20 x 7 mm). Glue one to the arrow.

14 Join the other two by gluing on a 0.2-inch (5-mm) wide rectangle. Shape this hinge around the skewer and fold back the wings.

15 Glue the double flight to the arrow shaft opposite the single flight.

Ready... Aim... Launch!

16 Pull back the rubber band with the arrow resting on one finger and the bow. Then launch!

THE MEDIEVAL LONGBOW

The English or Welsh longbow was typically 6 feet (1.8 m) long. Archers needed great strength and skill to draw and aim effectively. The longbow's maximum range was 1,300 feet (400 m) and it could penetrate plate armor from a distance of 320 feet (100 m).

CLOTHESPIN LAUNCHER

Secret agents need to know how to turn ordinary objects into spy weapons. Here's how to make a launcher from a wooden clothespin.

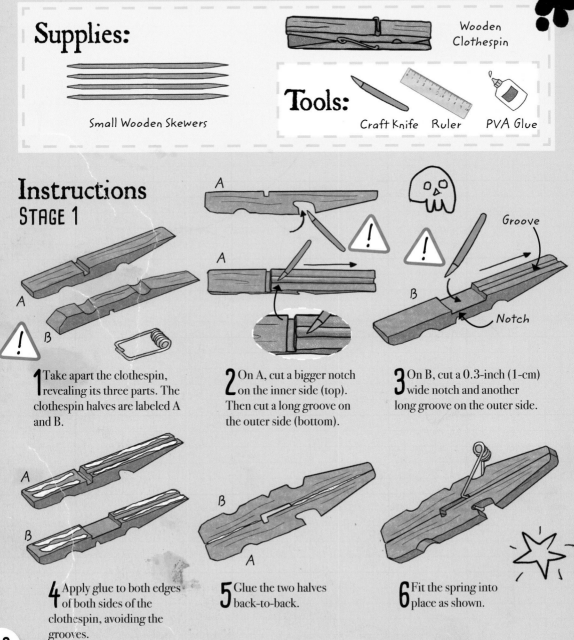

Supplies:

Small Wooden Skewers

Wooden Clothespin

Tools:

Craft Knife   Ruler   PVA Glue

Instructions
STAGE 1

1 Take apart the clothespin, revealing its three parts. The clothespin halves are labeled A and B.

2 On A, cut a bigger notch on the inner side (top). Then cut a long groove on the outer side (bottom).

3 On B, cut a 0.3-inch (1-cm) wide notch and another long groove on the outer side.

Groove

Notch

4 Apply glue to both edges of both sides of the clothespin, avoiding the grooves.

5 Glue the two halves back-to-back.

6 Fit the spring into place as shown.

STAGE 2

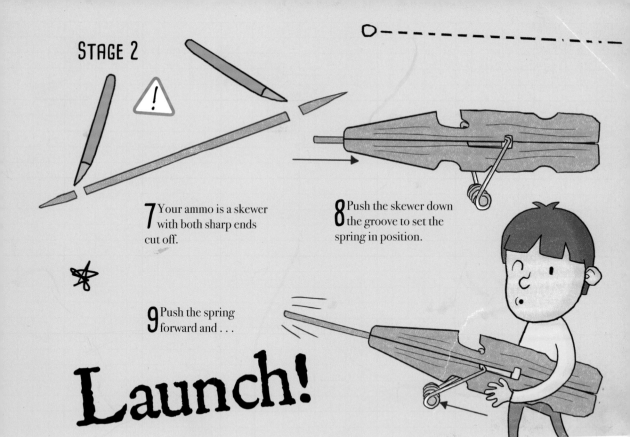

7 Your ammo is a skewer with both sharp ends cut off.

8 Push the skewer down the groove to set the spring in position.

9 Push the spring forward and . . .

Launch!

EARLY SPY WEAPONS

Miniature spy guns have been around for more than one hundred years. Some were designed to fit into a pocket or purse. Others masqueraded as a writing pen, a ring, a pocket watch, or a key. All could fit in the palm of the hand, or equally small space—and they worked.

CANDY LAUNCHER

This launcher sends candy mints flying through the air. It is based on a pistol with a boxlike magazine (container) for ammunition made by the famous German company Mauser.

Supplies:

Plastic Pen with Round Barrel
(wide enough for mints)

MINT

Large Wooden Skewer

Plastic Mint Box   **Mints**   **Rubber Bands x 2**

Tools:

Craft Knife   **Epoxy Glue**

Duct Tape   **Scissors**

Instructions
STAGE 1

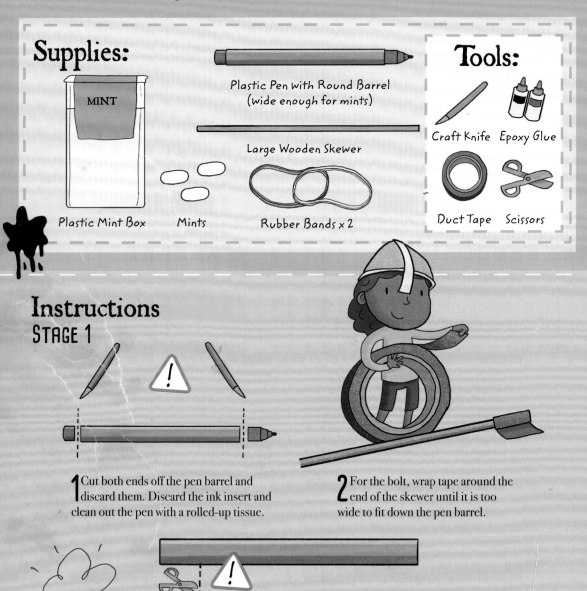

1 Cut both ends off the pen barrel and discard them. Discard the ink insert and clean out the pen with a rolled-up tissue.

2 For the bolt, wrap tape around the end of the skewer until it is too wide to fit down the pen barrel.

3 Cut the skewer to make it the same length as the barrel, including its taped end.

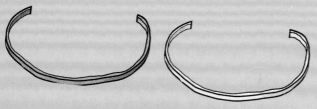

4 Cut two rubber bands and find their halfway points.

5 Fold the rubber band pieces over the taped end of the bolt and tape the pieces in place.

STAGE 2

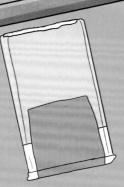

6 Glue the barrel to the bottom edge of the mint box. Don't eat all the mints—they will be your ammo. Make sure the mint box is upside down so you can load it later. The mint box makes the launcher's handle.

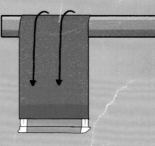

7 Tape over the barrel and handle with duct tape, leaving the box opening clear.

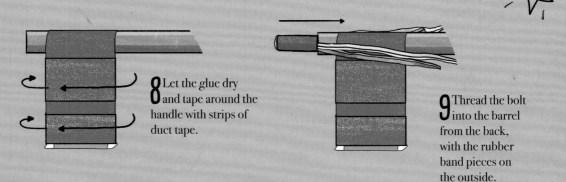

8 Let the glue dry and tape around the handle with strips of duct tape.

9 Thread the bolt into the barrel from the back, with the rubber band pieces on the outside.

10 Stretch the rubber band pieces along either side of the barrel and tape the pieces into position, leaving the ends free.

11 Fold the rubber band pieces back over the tape.

12 Tape them down to complete the bolt.

13 Drop a mint into the barrel.

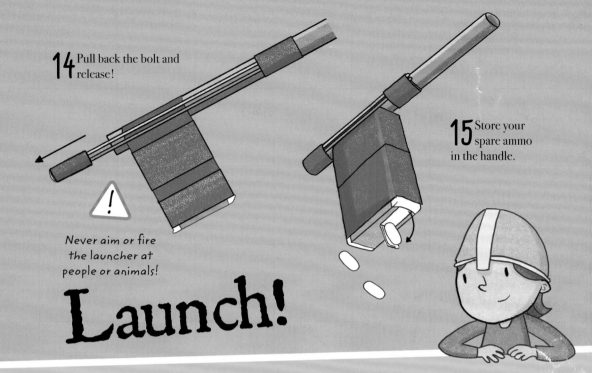

14 Pull back the bolt and release!

⚠️ Never aim or fire the launcher at people or animals!

15 Store your spare ammo in the handle.

Launch!

THE MAUSER

Also known as the "Broomhandle" because of its rounded wooden handle, the Mauser pistol was popular with army officers as a personal side arm. It was made from 1896 to 1937 and used in World War I (1914–1918).

THE FINISHED LAUNCHERS

These amazing models are based on historical weapons that launched projectiles in different ways. They might be used by a single warrior or whole army units.

Crayon Launcher

Based On: Medieval Crossbow

Invented In: Ancient China

Original Size: Variable, but usually up to 3 feet (9 m)

Paper Dart Launcher

Based On: Hunting Blowpipe

Invented In: South America and southeast Asia

Original Size: Up to 23 feet (7 m)

Rubber Band Launcher

Based On: Flintlock Pistol

Invented In: France

Original Size: 6–20 inches (15–50 cm)

Exploding Ninja Star

Based On: Japanese Shuriken

Invented In: Japan

Original Size: Up to 4 inches (10 cm)

Rocket Launcher

Based On: Japanese Bohiya (Fire Arrow) Launcher

Invented In: Ancient China

Original Size: Arrow, around 20 inches (50 cm)

Laminated Bow

Based On: Longbow

Invented In: Northern Europe

Original Size: 4–7 feet (1.2–2.1 m)

Clothespin Launcher

Based On: Nineteenth-century spy mini-weapons

Invented In: United States and Europe

Original Size: Variable, up to 4 inches (10 cm)

Candy Launcher

Based On: Mauser Pistol

Invented In: Germany

Original Size: Close to 10 inches (25 cm)

Small Weapons in History

Many early launchers remained in use for centuries because they were effective and accurate.

Raining Arrows

After years of training and practice, an archer would be able to shoot an arrow from his longbow every five seconds. Hundreds of archers together unleashed a whole rainstorm of arrows. At the Battle of Crécy in 1346, the French outnumbered the English by three to one. But English bowmen won the field.

Poison Darts

The Matis people of western Brazil make blowpipes from seven strips of palm bound together. They use the tooth of a capybara, the world's largest rodent, as a sight to help in aiming. Their darts are palm stems tipped with poison from the curare vine. They scrape the vine using a stick embedded with monkey teeth, and boil the mixture in water for two weeks.

Micro Spy

One important point about being a spy is that you mustn't appear to be one! For this reason a spy's weapons also had to pretend to be something else, and usually were very tiny. So, cuff links might be hollow with a mini-device inside. Or a chain attached to a nineteenth-century pocket watch might have a decorative fob that was a weapon rather than a lucky charm.

Lethal Weapon

The crossbow needed no special skill or strength to aim and fire. But the bolts struck enemies with deadly force. They inflicted such horrible wounds that one medieval pope tried to ban the weapon—unsuccessfully. While reloading on the battlefield, a crossbowman ducked behind his tall shield. A whole row of these formed a defensive screen called a *pavisade*.

INDEX

THE AUTHOR
Rob Ives is a United Kingdom-based designer and paper engineer.
He began making cardboard models as a math and science teacher,
and then was asked to create two books of models. His published
titles include *Paper Models that Rock!* and *Paper Automata*. He
specializes in paper animations and projects, and often visits schools
to talk about design technology and demonstrate his models.

THE ARTIST
John Paul de Quay is an illustrator with a BSc in Biology from
the University of Sussex, United Kingdom, and a postgraduate
certificate in animation from the University of the West of England.
He devotes his spare time to growing chili peppers, perfecting his
plan for a sustainable future, and caring for a small plastic dinosaur.
He has three pet squid that live in the bath, which makes drawing in
ink quite economical . . .